PSYCHOLOGICAL ASSESSMENTS AND THE PRIESTLY AND RELIGIOUS FORMATION PROCESS: MYTHS AND FACTS

Angela A. Egbikuadje, Ph. D.

Psychological Assessments and the Priestly and Religious
Formation Process: Myths and Facts

Copyright © 2013 by Angela A. Egbikuadje, Ph.D.
Email: metitiri1986@yahoo.com

Printed and bound in the United States of America.

ISBN-10: 0989277313

ISBN-13: 978-0989277310

Contents

Preface

During my religious formation years in Nigeria, there were rumors that some of the candidates in formation were sent home or refused their first vows based on the result of psychological tests. On that ground therefore, it became quite easy for many of us to not only critic the validity of such reports, but also to view the psychological testing process as one of "those" negative practices that formators use to support their sometimes illogical and irrational concepts of individuals in formation. For many years and albeit the different perceptions on the validity or reliability of psychological testing and the formation process, I have continued to embark on research on the psychological testing process. With my own personal experience as a test taker undergoing psychological tests and upon receipt of my own reports, my bias and myths on the testing process became completely invalidated. Although it is not my goal to change anyone's perceptions on the psychological testing process, it is my hope that readers will be more enlightened on the process and the benefits of psychological tests after reading this book.

This book will be beneficial to both formators and those in formation. The author selected some of the major myths of psychological testing as it relates specifically to the priestly and religious formation process and attempts to disprove the mistaken beliefs by addressing the facts of the testing process. On account of the readers and to ensure the clarity of the message, this book has been written in clear and simple language, avoiding all psychological jargons. However, documents of the Catholic Church such as the Post-Synodal Apostolic Exhortation *Pastores Dabo Vobis* and the International Guidelines for Test Use were fundamental to clarifying the different controversies regarding psychological testing and the priestly and religious formation in Africa.

It is an established fact that vocation to the priesthood or to the consecrated life is a special gift from God and the results of psychological tests do not in any way contradict such strong truth. It is not an expected practice either for formators to rely solely on the results of psychological tests during their selection process. Therefore, in this book, the author attempts to provide answers to some of the vital questions that formators, seminarians, novices, and aspirants have on the significance of psychological tests and how it complements their gift of vocation. Furthermore, this book also offers more light by providing the readers with more information on the meaning of strength-based psychological assessments and how it positively impacts the priestly or religious in formation and their overall selection process.

<u>**MYTH #1...**</u>

Psychological testing is a Western culture practice; therefore the testing instruments cannot be utilized with African populations.

Facts

1. The practice of psychological testing has extended beyond the Western word.

2. The psychological test administration process, the interpretation of psychological tests results, and the use of the psychological test results are guided by the International Test Commission (ITC, 2000), an association whose members include African organizations.

3. Psychological tests results must be interpreted in a manner that does not ignore the test taker's cultural, family, spiritual, educational, medical, and other relevant psychosocial values and norms.

The use of psychological tests results depend to a large extent on the reason for the psychological testing as well as other factors. No one contests the fact that psychological assessments are imperfect and do not alone provide a true picture of the test taker. However, the degree to which psychological tests results are justified and usable depends on factors such as the psychologist's level of education, knowledge and experience in psychological testing, and knowledge about psychological testing research. The psychologist administering psychological testing must have the following qualifications:

- Experience in the actual administration, scoring, and interpretation of the tests
- Knowledge of the acceptable ethical standards for the use of psychological testing in different cultures
- Knowledge of the impact of the test takers' psycho-socio-cultural background on the different test instruments that is administered.

Furthermore and of greater relevance, the *International Guidelines for Test Use* (ITC, 2000) emphasize that psychologists administering psychological tests possess the following qualities:

- Knowledge and understanding of the relevant theories and models of cognition
- Knowledge of the different personality profiles and psychopathologies

- Knowledge and experience in integrating intellectual abilities, cognition, and different personality profiles in both the choice of tests and the interpretation of their results
- Knowledge and experience in interpreting tests results objectively using both formal and informal data such as biographical data, unstructured interviews, references, and more.

No doubt, the practice of psychological testing in Africa has ethical dilemmas. No matter where psychological tests are administered, the administering psychologists cannot take for granted their sensitivity to the test takers' cultural backgrounds and values as they select the tests and interpret the test results (Foxcroft, 2002). Notwithstanding, the reliability of any psychological test results is contingent upon the test taker's responses to the administered tests (Wilkinson & Task Force on Statistical Inference, 1999). Therefore, psychologists administering tests must inform the test takers, including seminarians and individuals aspiring to different religious congregations, of the importance of furnishing objective, valid, and truthful responses during the psychological testing process.

The use of different psychological testing instruments helps minimize errors in interpretation and the use of tests results. Basically, projective assessment instruments complement structured questionnaire instruments so that the presence of any psychological trait or serious psychiatric illness is not overlooked. The administration of different psychological tests measuring similar traits is necessary to reduce discrepancies among the different test results relating to information about the presence of any pathology or personality trait. For example, for personality assessments focusing on identifying the presence of psychopathology or serious psychiatric conditions, the use of both projective and objective tests are encouraged.

The combination of the results of the projective and objective tests, as well as the integration of the results of the unstructured personal interview, behavioral observations, and other histories, helps to mitigate the popular belief that psychological test results cannot be applied to African populations. Nevertheless, one cannot overemphasize the ongoing need for psychometrics and psychologists to improve on norming more psychological instruments to African populations. Such norming only makes the testing instruments more reliable and of greater validity. In the *Inter-*

national Guidelines for Test Use (ITC, 2000), psychologists are expected to use test instruments that are unbiased and have appropriate documentation on their validity, relevancy, and reliability.

The applicability of psychological test instruments to African populations relies greatly on the interpretation of the test results. Psychologists need to consider how different mental and personality disorders are manifested in different cultures. For example, a Nigerian with schizophrenia will generally present with symptoms of confusion, bizarre delusions, and disorganized behavior. A Nigerian adult who is depressed might present with symptoms such as frequent anger outbursts, irritability, increased fears, low frustration tolerance, tearfulness, and difficulties with sleep. This might differ for people who hail from other cultures or countries.

Although specific symptoms are linked to different disorders including schizophrenia and depression or anxiety, what is paramount is that the presentation of the different symptoms of a psychiatric disorder or personality dysfunction varies from one culture to another and from one individual to the other within the same culture. Therefore the psychologist administering a psychological test must conduct a clinical interview with the test taker in order to produce a reliable and valid result. A good clinical interview includes, but is not limited to, questions that explore the social, educational, family, mental health, physical health, spiritual/religious, cultural, and developmental history of the test taker. Observations of the behavior of the test taker during these clinical interviews provide additional information that makes the report more complete. The ITC (2000) *International Guidelines for Test Use* requires that psychologists administering psychological tests in diverse populations "avoid over-generalizing the results of one test to traits or human characteristics which are not measured by the test" (p. 5). They must "be aware of the negative social stereotyping that may pertain to members of the test taker's group (e.g., cultural group, age, social class, and gender)." (p. 5).

Choosing Psychological Tests:
The Referral Question

Having established that psychological tests can be administered and interpreted in the African culture, the need remains to point out the relevance of having an appropriate referral question. The administration of psychological tests to seminarians, novices, or those preparing to join the priesthood or consecrated life must have a purpose and a specific referral question. The choice of tests used for psychological assessment depends on the referral question. However, researchers have recommended that both objective and projective tests be used for individuals pursuing the priestly and religious vocation (McGlone et al., 2010; Plante & Boccaccini, 1998). A clear and focused referral question allows the psychologist to choose psychological test instruments that are appropriate. Wolber and Carne (2002) observed, "Not addressing the referral question is ignoring the referent's perceived needs and may result not only in a misguided report but also in ill feelings between the referent and the report writer" (p. 3). Following the contents of the referral question, the psychologist chooses psychological tests instruments that best answer the referral question. More so, the relevance of the test takers' compliance is clarified when referral questions are succinct and discussed.

Furthermore, evidence-based psychological assessment measures provide individuals in formation a deeper knowledge and understanding of their personality and better insight into the formation process. Such assessments also permit individualization of the candidates' formation experiences so that resistances to proposals from their formators are minimized if not avoided (Grocholewski, 2008). With the referral question in mind, and after the administration of the psychological tests to the test taker, the psychologist is able to provide appropriate and the relevant feedback to the referral source.

Feedback Process:
Bishops, Seminary Authority, Formation
Team/Vocation Directors

No doubt, test results or reports are by no means sufficient for determining the personality or cognitive processes of any test taker. Ethical guidelines in the practice of cross-cultural psychology demand that psychological test results be viewed as part of the whole in the evaluation of the seminarian, the aspirant, or those preparing to enter the seminary or the novitiate. Poston and Hanson (2010) observed that psychological test results or reports are most beneficial when used in collaboration with other treatment and evaluation tools. The researchers suggested that the psychological test results would be most beneficial when the test taker is provided feedback from the psychological testing process and can use that feedback to alter behaviors or address troubling personality traits. The feedback process is most beneficial when the psychologist who administered the tests provides the feedback to the seminarian or individual aspiring to the consecrated life. Furthermore and most importantly, although the conclusions of the psychological report might be viewed sometimes as nothing more than possible hypotheses, when diagnosis of a serious pathology or mental health condition is part of the findings, the diagnosis is usually reliable and must be taken very seriously. The presence of a mental health condition might not be obvious to the formation authority and thus such a finding can create some controversy. When the accuracy of the finding is doubted, more tests batteries should be administered. Administration of psychological tests has been found to be the most reliable way to determine or confirm the presence of any serious mental health or psychiatric condition.

MYTH #2...

Psychological test results are used to label healthy and appropriately functioning individuals as mentally ill.

Facts

1. Psychological test instruments are diagnostic tools. Their results help to clarify or confirm either the presence or the absence of a cognitive, personality, or mental condition.

2. Psychological test results are explorative tools used to help individuals and families understand how they function and how they view themselves in comparison with others. Such exploration includes career assessment, occupational functioning assessment in the workplace, and emotional functioning assessment in stressful or non-stressful environments.

3. Psychological test results have been found to help individuals understand their strengths and weaknesses in relation to their social, work, school, and family environments.

4. Psychological test results have been used as preventive measures. The results of the tests can be used by the test taker or the testers to prevent the onset of psychological conditions. The results of the tests also serve as aids for improving self and behaviors.

The purpose of psychological assessments is to improve the psychological, social, educational, emotional, and physical functioning of the test taker. Unlike allowing individuals to obtain their laboratory results and not know what to do about them unless they return to their physicians, good psychological reports enable recipients to act on the information provided. Although mental or personality problems are not always diagnosed after completion of a psychological test, when they are identified the psychologist does not end the report with the diagnosis; rather, the psychologist always offers relevant suggestions on how the test taker might ameliorate the pathology or the symptoms of the pathology. The psychologist will not readily prescribe medications, especially when prescription privileges are not part of the psychologist duties. Even when psychiatric medications are obviously part of the recommendations for the test taker; the psychologist can in most cases provide other forms of treatment and if needed, the psychologist will also refer the patient to either a psychiatrist or to a clinical psychologist with prescription privileges.

In accordance with the international guidelines for tests use (ITC, 2000), psychologists must make every effort to avoid inflicting harm or causing unwarranted distress to test takers. To prevent any psychological harm or inappropriate diagnosis, psychologists must not only take care to use only tests they are qualified to administer, but they must also avoid creating wrong impressions or hypotheses as they interpret test results and reports. To provide a well-rounded psychological testing process, psychologists are not limited to assessing only the presence of significant mental health conditions; they may also use psychological tests instruments that help determine the specific strengths of the test taker.

Strength-based Assessments

Researchers such as Bird et al. (2012) have urged psychologists to include strength-based assessments as part of routine testing. Thus, irrespective of the referral question, more psychologists include strength-based assessment instruments in the batteries of tests they administer to seminarians and individuals aspiring to orders of consecrated lives. Strength-based approaches to psychological testing stem from the work of humanistic psychologists such as Carl Rogers and Abraham Maslow. These humanistic psychologists believed that "being human means being creative and that psychology must aim to help people live more creative lives" (Nevid, Rathus, & Greene, 1997, p. 57). They identified three different levels of strength-based assessments: individual, environmental, and interpersonal.

Moreover, the use of strength-based assessments has been identified as an evidence-based practice of positive psychology. Evidence-based practices of psychology such as the virtue ethics approach take test takers' values and ethics into careful consideration. In the virtue ethics approach to assessing strengths, strengths are viewed not only in terms of the test takers' values, but also on the moral content of goodness inherent in that value (Bird et al., 2012). The concept of goodness is relevant especially when the test taker presents with symptoms that meet criteria for a mental disorder, a problem behavior, or a personality problem. For example, a test taker with traits of a personality problem such as narcissistic personality disorder may possess the quality of being other-centered and have the capability of developing pleasurable and positive interpersonal relationships. In the ordinary sense, such an individual can be described as "full of himself and annoying but kind and social." The point here is that psychological assessment results must aim to present individuals seeking the priestly vocation or vocation to the consecrated life as capable of performing (not necessarily having performed) the tasks and meeting the challenges their job might entail in a manner that does not ignore their positive traits. The use of comprehensive and balanced assessment instruments has also been traced to the development of assessment instruments that center on emotional intelligence and the workplace.

Work Performance Assessments

Work performance assessments measure appropriate behaviors in the workplace. Just as the test takers' degree of appropriateness of behavior in the workplace predicts their performance, so also, the use of work performance assessments as well as assessing for emotional intelligence has grown over the last several decades. Work performance assessments do not usually focus on the presence of mental illness or any pathology, but on whether the test takers possess the skills necessary for performing their job tasks. Cook and Cripps (2005) explained that psychologists use work performance assessment instruments that measure the test takers' ability to follow the organization's instructions, learn and implement new skills in the job, and exhibit talent related to the job tasks. The researchers added that work performance tools must also be able to assess the test takers' ability to make sound judgments regarding fulfilling various planned and unplanned tasks required by their job and their ability to modulate or manage their temperament, interests, values, preferences, and perceptions in such a positive manner that their job tasks are not compromised.

Considering that Christian anthropology and good ethical practice demands that psychologists who include work performance assessments in the myriad of tests they administer understand their test takers beyond the information gathered from the test instruments, knowing the test takers makes the results of the psychological testing process more empirically accurate. In scholarly research conducted in 2010, McGlone, Ortiz, and Karney examined relationships between psychologists and test takers. The researchers explored the impact of the psychological assessment process on the admission of candidates to the priesthood in the United States Catholic Church. The majority of the psychologists in the study suggested that there should be a firm and honest relationship between the vocation director and the psychologist. To ensure the usefulness of the psychological testing results, the research participants also suggested that the psychologists involved in the testing process are able to integrate the following: their understanding of the Catholic formation process, their assessment of the ability of the individuals in formation to fulfill their religious vocations, and their knowledge of the different observed psychological functioning or traits as they interpret and complete the psychological reports. These research participants also indicated that the psychological assessments of individuals aspiring to be priests, religious, or other types of consecrated persons must take into consideration the candidates' affective maturity, which is also broadly known as emotional intelligence.

Assessments of Emotional Intelligence

Affective maturity, or emotional intelligence, simply refers to an individual's ability to conveniently show effective control of their feelings. The feelings, whether overt or covert, significantly affect the individual's interpersonal relationships. Knowing full well that priests, religious, and consecrated individuals will be persons of authority upon ordination or entering their profession and that their roles involve work with different kinds of people, the ecclesiastical authority and/or superiors are not only urged to recognize the strong need for psychological assessments for those in formation, but assessments that include assessments of affective maturity. Additionally, the fact that priests, religious or consecrated persons experience loneliness in ministry is a major reason that those who aspire to these vocations attain an appropriate level of affective maturity while in formation (John Paul II, 1992). Although the absence of affective maturity does not necessarily mean individuals are not capable of fulfilling their assigned ministry duties, individuals who have not achieved affective maturity are likely to have difficulty in relations with their authority, their peers, and those they serve. A lack in affective maturity signifies a lack of love. As John Paul II explained, "Affective maturity presupposes an awareness that love has a central role in human life... love that involves the entire person. physical, psychic, and spiritual.... which is expressed in the 'nuptial meaning' of the human body" (p. 43).

Psychologically, for an individual lacking in affective maturity, dealing with stress, changes, conflict, and disorganization is more challenging. Self-esteem and self-concepts are elements of affective maturity, and they need to be upheld. Moreover, individuals planning to participate in priestly, religious, or consecrated formation are expected to understand the true meaning of their vocation and be humble enough to address those areas in their human self that are deficient in affective maturity. The humility of priests or consecrated persons in formation in terms of their acceptance of imperfection is yet another facet of affective maturity that has a significant impact on their ability to remain dedicated to their calling. Besides, the practice of humility is sacred and can be observed in communications in the church's hierarchy. Psychologically, humble communications are viewed as positive interactional skills that do not only promote a positive social environment, but heightens' the individual's affective maturity.

Communication and
Psychological Assessment

Assessment of communication skills, particularly assessment using psychological instruments, is not regularly conducted in Africa. Nevertheless, formation teams need to understand the importance of effective communication to the fulfillment of assigned tasks during and upon completion of the formation process. A major drawback to the use of appropriate psychological instruments for assessing effective communication skills is the cost of the psychological testing materials. Nonetheless, when the referral question involves the need to assess for communication abilities, the psychologist must endeavor to perform such tests using the appropriate instruments. When tests are unavailable, the psychologists should include in the assessment report the reason for the lapse.

The nature of the role of priests, religious, and consecrated in Africa, which includes evangelism, makes effective communication skills necessary. Communication skills are both verbal and non-verbal; they are related to the cognitive functioning of the individual. Communication skills are not limited to an individual's ability to verbally express or respond to what is being communicated to them verbally or in writing. Effective communication involves the individual's ability to effectively utilize their critical reasoning faculties; which in fact is one determinant of responsible behavior. Responsible behavior is a measure of both an individual's ability to effectively implement the instructions that is being communicated to them as well as their ability to utilize their critical reasoning skills when they attempt to fulfill tasks communicated to them. The measure of critical reasoning skills is integrated into most psychological assessments of intellectual functioning. If the results of the psychological testing for any individual show a lack of effective communication skills, the psychologist recommends a process through which that individual can learn to communicate more effectively and most especially improve on their critical reasoning abilities. Communication skills are affected by both environmental and cultural factors as well. Therefore, the cognitive abilities of the test takers, their problem solving skills, and their rational behavior characteristics are measured during the psychological assessment process. To add, the absence of effective communication skills does not mean the presence of a mental disorder or a serious pathology, but simply imply that the individual lacks the skills necessary for maintaining effective communication. However, it is pertinent for formators and the individuals in formation to note that the lack of effective communication has been found to be the major underlying factor in most conflicts between leaders and their subordinates and between individuals of the same category. Thus, when psychological tests results show problems with effective communication, the formators, as well as the individual in formation should take it seriously. The results of psychological assessments that focuses on effective communication is meant to enhance the personality of the individual in formation and the practice of effective communication skills can never go unrewarded.

Psychological Assessment and Individuals in Formation

Test takers and those in the formation team should view the results of psychological assessments as means for fostering growth in individuals. This perspective is predicated on the understanding that individuals can mature in the vocation they received from God and psychological reports are added resources for the candidates in their vocational journey (Grocholewski, 2008). Seminarians in formation and those aspiring to other religious or consecrated vocations should use psychological assessments to see their strengths as talents to be shared and their weakness as areas in which to improve. When the assessments uncover serious psychopathology (e.g., personality problems, poor cognitive processing skills, behavior problems, etc.), those in authority are required to help the seminarian or the religious seek professional help immediately. Where there is doubt, psychological assessments can be repeated using different instruments. Timely discernment and intervention for any candidate in formation presenting with psychic disturbances, affective immaturity, or other psychological issues are highly recommended (Grocholewski).

MYTH #3...

The psychological testing process is both an attempt to "weed" out people from the seminary and the novitiate and an avenue for allowing discriminatory practices in the selection process.

Facts

1. The use of psychological test instruments and results is not restricted to institutions of the Catholic Church; it is widespread in hospitals, schools and educational settings, the workplace, the courts, and other forensic settings. Psychological tests assess the cognitive, intellectual, and personality functioning of individuals.

2. Psychological test results benefit individuals seeking holistic growth in their personalities. Educational institutions use psychological test results to help students achieve excellence, and psychological test results enable employers to identify employees committed to good performance and high productivity.

3. The psychologist's duties do not include membership on the seminary or novitiate formation team.

The psychologist's role is either advisory or consultative only.

Psychological Tests, Catholic Church Documents, and the Test User

The Catholic Church has established regulations regarding the administration and the use of psychological tests results in Africa. The regulations and guidelines can be found in the documents of the Second Vatican Council, canon law, Catholic bishops' conferences, the Congregation for Catholic Education, and apostolic exhortations. The call to the priesthood or the religious or consecrated life is a special gift from God, and the use of psychological science in examining fitness for the call does not minimize the underlying principles of this special gift of total consecration. Psychological testing "allows a more sure evaluation of the candidate's psychic state; it can help evaluate his human dispositions for responding to the divine call, and it can provide some assistance for the candidate's human growth" (Grocholewski, 2008, p. 3). Irrespective of the fact that the strength and benefit of any psychological test relies greatly on how well it is used (Anastasi, 1992), psychologists have guidelines regarding how to communicate test results to the referral source. Similarly, the test user who is competent and ethical must "use tests appropriately, professionally, and in an ethical manner, paying due regard to the needs and rights of those involved in the testing process, the reasons for the testing, and the broader context in which the testing takes place" (ITC, 2000, p. 6). Test users are required to use psychological tests results objectively and in collaboration with other evaluative records.

To ensure the unbiased use of test results, the clinical psychologist must educate vocation directors about the different psychological profiles and how they impact the ability of priests and religious to continue in formation and consequently fulfill their ministerial tasks. Psychologists must effectively communicate the results of the psychological testing to the referral source. Because the vocations director or the relevant vocation team members may not be very knowledgeable about the differences between the different personalities and the cognitive and emotional functioning of any test taker, psychologists need to avoid using difficult language and psychological jargon in their reports. Psychologists must not only present the report in very clear language, but they must also provide feedback in such a manner that it is constructive, supportive, and within the context of the referral question (ITC, 2000). Depending on the diocese and the needs of the diocese in terms of psychological assessments of the individuals pursuing the priestly vocation or the vocation to the religious or consecrated life, it might be necessary to have a structured form or protocol for reporting the results of psychological assessments. The disadvantage of structured forms or protocols is that they sometimes limit the degree to which a psychologist can include relevant information not on the forms. Consequently, the best way to receive beneficial results from psychological testing is for the vocations director to present the psychologist with a good referral question and the psychologist to provide a report that endeavors to answer the referral question and includes the rationale for the conclusions reached.

Furthermore, the formators have the responsibility of using the psychological reports as guidelines for creating the type, steps, and path of formation required for the candidates seeking ordination to the priesthood or entrance to other forms of consecrated life (Grocholewski, 2008). Finally, clinical psychologists or assessment practitioners in Africa must have a firm and accurate understanding of their purpose and communicate that purpose to the referral source prior to commencing the psychological testing. Clinical psychologists conducting psychological assessments in cultural settings or countries different from those in which the assessments were developed or normed must "be alert to any unintended consequences of test use" (ITC, 2000, p. 10) and make all reasonable efforts to secure the test documents and materials to avoid any unauthorized access (ITC, 2000).

Confidentiality and Psychological Assessments

One of the ethical responsibilities of the clinical psychologist is to maintain confidentiality. With the understanding that confidentiality is not restricted to the clinical psychologist and the test taker, the test taker needs to be educated on the informed consent procedure prior to beginning the psychological assessment process. It is good ethical practice for psychologists conducting psychological testing with individuals seeking the priestly and religious vocations to have both verbal and written informed consent. Informed consent means informing the test taker who will have access to the psychological reports, the primary person to whom the reports will be released, and the form (verbal or written) in which the psychological reports will be released. For individuals pursuing the priestly vocation, the bishops of the diocese, the vocation directors, and the seminary formation team might be authorized recipients of the psychological reports; for individuals aspiring to orders of consecrated lives, their superiors, vocation directors, formation directresses or directors, and members of the formation team are authorized recipients of the psychological reports. Although dictating who has access to the psychological testing reports is out of the psychologist's scope of practice, it is important that the psychologist send the psychological reports to the vocation director (or referral source) who has submitted a formal referral request. Although legal consequences are rare in African societies, it is also good ethical practice for psychologists to request that test takers sign a waiver releasing the results of the psychological testing to the individual(s) identified on the informed consent form.

To further validate the informed consent process, formators and those in formation should maintain a cordial relationship and open communication characterized by transparency and truthfulness. Cordial relationships and open communication keep the psychological consultation process from being viewed as a means to support the dismissal of a student from the formation process (Grocholewski, 2008). According to the ITC (2000), the signed informed consent of the test taker enables the psychologist to produce written and oral reports. As a matter of emphasis, the Catholic Church has stated that psychological assessment of candidates to the priesthood or of those in priestly formation "must always be carried out with the previous, explicit, informed and free consent of the candidate" (Grocholewski, p. 4). Furthermore, although not the norm, psychological assessments might be requested when there is "doubt concerning the candidate's suitability" for admission to the seminary or house of formation (Grocholewski, p. 7). Irrespective of the circumstances that precede the request for the psychological test, the test taker is expected to sign the informed consent in the spirit of reciprocal trust. Such trust may be validated only when the test taker is allowed access to the psychological test results.

Generally, the manner in which the results are reported is important. The psychologists who administer the tests need to allow their clients ample opportunity to ask questions or request clarification on subjects or areas that are unclear to them. Psychologists who utilize effective communication skills as they discuss tests results assure that test takers have a good understanding of their results and what the results indicate.

Communicating Tests Results
to the Test Taker

Psychologists have differing views regarding discussing the results of psychological tests with test takers. Some psychologists support the practice of meeting with test takers in individual sessions for the purpose of discussing the test results, noting the benefits to the test taker of understanding the results. Others discourage discussion of the results, focusing on the risks associated with disclosure of the information. Despite the different ethical points of view on the issue of communicating the results of psychological testing in general, in the specific case of individuals in priestly formation or aspiring to be consecrated in a religious congregation, discussion of psychological reports with the test taker is important. With individuals seeking priestly or religious vocations, the focus is on the benefits rather than the risks. When psychologists share test results with the test takers, the level of stress in the test taker is reduced, there is increased willingness on the part of the test taker to be optimistic, and there is increased motivation and positive attitude towards the testing process and its purpose (McGlone et al., 2010 and Poston & Hanson, 2010). What is most relevant is the test takers' desire for growth and improvement of their knowledge of self after receiving testing feedback. To reiterate, strength-based assessment helps individuals recognize their strengths, improve on their weaknesses, and remain humble as they utilize their strengths or talents in their service of God to humanity.

MYTH #4...

The psychological testing process downplays the true meaning of the priestly and religious vocation -- which is a gift from God and a calling that is firmly rooted in spirituality and religion.

Fact

Psychological testing involves the use of evidence-based practice instruments to assess areas of human functioning that are psychologically predisposed.

Psychological Testing and the Gift of Vocation

Psychological testing involves the comprehensive evaluation of human functioning, including the intellect, cognitive processes, personality, and emotional functioning. For individuals in the priestly or religious formation process in the Catholic Church, the church requires that the "assistance offered by the psychological sciences must be integrated within the context of the candidate's entire formation. It must not obstruct, but rather ensure, in a particular way that the irreplaceable value of spiritual accompaniment is guaranteed" (Grocholewski, 2008, pp. 4-5). Furthermore, the guidelines the church has established for the use of psychological testing reports in the admission and formation of candidates for the priesthood or religious vocation, includes the following information (Grocholewski):

1. The fact that the vocation to the priesthood is a special gift from God does not preclude the usefulness of psychological testing for evaluating the human elements inherent in the person responding to the divine call.

2. Ruling out "psychic" disturbances and other serious pathologies in the individual responding to the divine call to the priesthood is necessary if ministries are to be effectively completed after the ordination to the priesthood or completion of religious profession.

3. Being human implies the presence of some strengths and weaknesses. Considering the multifaceted nature of the different ministries of the ordained priests and religious, talents and weakness

need to be explored to fostering the growth of the church.

4. Balance between the human self and the spiritual self and the development of living in human form what is being communicated from the spiritual self are important for priests and religious to exercise their assigned ministries. Psychological testing instruments can be used to evaluate personality constructs that might hinder or promote such balance and development. Psychological problems, whether interpersonal, intrapsychic, spiritual, educational, or occupational, can impact the overall functioning of any person. Within the West African collectivistic culture, family conflicts that hinder the psychological functioning of candidates for the priesthood can be devastating to the spiritual self of candidates seeking the priestly or religious vocation. Conflicts resulting from family instability need to be resolved amicably because of their negative ramification on emotions and interpersonal relationships.

5. The psychologist is never part of the formation team. The role of the psychologist is properly viewed as nothing more than that of a professional

expert in clarifying human personalities and the overall psychological functioning of the human person. Psychologists chosen to perform psychological tests on candidates for spiritual vocations must have sound spiritual and human maturity, must understand the mystery of humans and how people interact with God and the church, and must understand the Catholic vocation of the priesthood and the celibate lifestyle.

6. Psychological reports are to be integrated into the formation process and in no way do psychological sciences replace the spiritual atmosphere of prayer, meditation, and the study of the word of God. Moreover, it is the responsibility of each country's formation team and religious authorities to regulate the use of psychological reports in terms of how they are used to promote the growth of the human person striving to become a priest or religious/consecrated.

Evidence-based Practice and Psychological Science

Science has been integral to the development of psychological test instruments as tools of evidence-based practice just as in the medical field testing the usefulness or reliability of any medication requires measuring both the placebo effect and the actual treatment effect. The foundations of psychological testing instruments are the theories behind the different psychological constructs such as personality, intellect, vocation, and emotional functioning (McFall, 2005). Psychological testing instruments are normed according to scientific procedures, and they include spirituality and religion as basic components of the human person. The selection of the different psychological test measures involves serious, thorough, and careful evaluation of the different theories that apply to the constructs being measured. The validity of psychological testing instruments is established by taking into consideration scientifically proven presentations for the different traits or constructs being measured (e.g., depression, anxiety, learning disability, schizophrenia, autism). Extensive use of statistical analysis with a broad group of volunteers helps to determine the

43

reliability and validity of the psychological test instruments. As the careful creation, refinement, and validation of the psychological instruments indicate, the focus of each instrument is the construct that is measured.

Whether individuals' religious and spiritual foundations will impact the test results depends to a large extent on how the individuals approach the testing process, what the test questions are, and how the individuals respond. Spirituality, religion, attitudes, and an individual's moral values have similar effects on psychological tests. Consequently, clinical psychologists with training and experience in testing individuals from different cultural and religious backgrounds will take into consideration the cultural and moral values of the test takers as they interpret the test results. For example, on a personality assessment test such as the MMPI-2 or MCMI-2, an individual pursuing the priestly vocation or vocation to the consecrated/religious life might present as free of flaws or free of any moral deficit. In such an instance, which is actually quite common, the psychologist interpreting the test results will proceed with caution. Instead of drawing a quick conclusion that the test taker is narcissistic, a liar, or attempting to hide their weaknesses or idiosyncrasies, the psychologist considers information from the clinical interview of the test taker, clinical observations, and the results of the other psychological instruments administered for the same purpose.

Evidence-based practice measures such as psychological testing instruments have been found to accurately describe individuals from a variety of cultural backgrounds. There is no doubt however, that clarifying the purposes and methods of psychological testing as well as the testing instruments for seminarians or religious in formation is a dynamic process. Human behavior is a function of the environment in which the humans operate, and environments change. Psychologist are therefore reminded to interpret tests results following the specific test guidelines; as well as taking into consideration, the cultural background of the test taker, the complexities of human growth, and other dynamic environmental or social factors.

Psychological Testing and Growth
Of the Individual in Formation

The role of psychological assessments in spiritual formation is to foster the growth of the priest or religious in formation. The formation process for priests and religious addresses four areas: human, spiritual, intellectual, and pastoral (John Paul II, 1992). In his Post-Synodal apostolic exhortation to the bishops, clergy, and faithful on the formation of priests, Pope John Paul II identified the underlying factor in the priestly formation as the human factor; the pope exhorted the priest in formation to "mold his human personality in such a way that it becomes a bridge and not an obstacle for others in their meeting with Jesus Christ the Redeemer of humanity" (p. 42). Furthermore, the pope observed, the capacity of priests or religious to form positive relationships; to remain sensitive to the needs of others and to society's problems; to promote justice and integrity; to communicate effectively; and to exercise sound, discreet, and fair judgment demands a balanced human quality. Psychological assessments are useful in helping candidates achieve that balance, facilitating improvement of the individual's ability to relate to other people, the community, and the society at large.

MYTH #5...

Psychological assessment results are never truly representative of any person. They are nothing but biased speculations and assumptions about how people operate.

Facts

1. Psychology is a science. Just as in the field of medicine medications are prescribed following specific guidelines, the effectiveness of psychological assessments lie in the psychologist's knowledge, competence, and experience in following specific test guidelines, policies, and procedures during the administration of the tests, the interpretation of the test data, and the presentation of objective psychological reports.

2. Psychological reports are an integration of objective records, subjective information (e.g., clinical interview or history from the client), and statistical analysis of the test taker's responses on different tests instruments. The clinical expertise of the psychologist, who understands the different traits being

47

measured, enables the psychologist to integrate the relevant data to produce objective report that include hypotheses, diagnoses, strengths and weaknesses, as well as recommendations.

3. Psychology recognizes the different developmental stages of the human person and how they impact the person's view of self and the person's social, behavioral, mental, educational, psychological, physical, and spiritual functioning. Consequently, the psychological assessment results are interpreted with the understanding of the developmental stage of the unique test taker in mind.

4. The role of the psychologist is not to make decisions on who is qualified to continue in priestly or religious formation. A major goal of psychological reports is to assist people to understand themselves more accurately and broadly, appreciate themselves for who they are, help them to grow where growth is needed, and help them to function more maturely at their developmental level.

Changing Psychological Profiles

It is not unusual for the psychological profile of individuals to change 4 or 5 years after initial psychological testing. The reason for the change does not lie in the myth that the psychological reports are nothing but speculations, but in the fact that change is part of life. Human maturity or growth is a function of several environmental factors such as increased social and family responsibility, experiences of tragedy or trauma, influence of peers and people in authority, educational growth, spiritual growth, better understanding of self and improved self-concept, advancement in age, and more. The degree to which the psychological profiles of individuals change varies. The psychological profiles of some people do not change considerably. The presence of significant pathologies such as psychotic symptoms (schizophrenia), bipolar disorder symptoms (e.g., irrational money spending habits, inability to sleep for days, sexual promiscuity, etc.), problematic personality qualities (e.g. sexual dysfunction, sexual identity problems, pedophilic tendencies, borderline, narcissistic, antisocial, or dependent personality qualities, addiction tendencies, etc.) usually remains unchanged once identified using evidence-based practice measures. However, stating categorically that individuals with certain mental illnesses, developmental problems, learning problems, or personality dysfunctions cannot live a good life in African society is flawed. The ability of such individuals to function successfully in society depends on their willingness to continually address their psychological problems and take the steps necessary to follow through with prescribed treatment strategies.

When psychological reports identify significant pathologies in any candidate to the priesthood or religious life, it is up to the members of the formation team to determine whether to risk allowing candidates with significant pathologies to continue in the formation program. To re-emphasize, the role of the psychologist is never to make decisions regarding retention or dismissal for the referral source; rather the role of the psychologist is to provide a psychological report based on scientific data and to offer expert/factual recommendations and suggestions only when appropriate or consulted.

However, the formation team and the individual in formation have a great advantage when defects in personality are detected early. Early detection of defects in the individual exploring the priestly vocation or aspiring to the consecrated or religious life enables the formation team and the individual in formation to avoid tragic situations or experiences that might follow if the defects had gone undetected. Furthermore, when defects, such as emotional immaturity are detected early, it is the role of the formators to assist individuals in formation to achieve the necessary emotional maturity commensurate with their calling (Sacred Congregation for Catholic Education, 1974).

Developmental Process and the Candidates in Formation

The human person goes through different stages of development over their lifetime. Although it is not my intention to bore you with the different phases of development, it is essential for members of the formation team to understand that certain behavioral characteristics, psychological and emotional maturity, and physiological features can be attributed to the different developmental stages. Individuals who lack the characteristics typical of a specific developmental stage are viewed as not meeting the milestones of that developmental stage. For example, children are expected to walk and talk at some point within certain age ranges; a child who fails to accomplish these tasks within the expected age range is not meeting the developmental milestones associated with that stage. Another example of failure to meet developmental milestone is a 25-year-old person with behavioral and emotional characteristics of a 12- year-old. However, the inability to meet one's developmental milestones in a timely manner does not preclude success in life. With early and appropriate psychological and sometimes physiological interventions, individuals who are slow in meeting their developmental milestones sometimes improve significantly.

Developmental Stages and
Changing Psychological Profiles

A change in a person's psychological profile over time does not necessarily indicate the absence of symptoms or a biased report. Changes in certain aspects of the human person are to be expected when tests are repeated after 3 or more years. It is not uncommon to hear people say: "Two years ago my reaction would have been different." Psychology is a science that recognizes the evolving and dynamic nature of human development, growth, and functioning.

Psychology also takes into consideration that human development is not static and human behavior is a product of the individuals' environments and their cognitive processing skills. Developmental theorists such as Jean Piaget, Erik Erikson, Sigmund Freud, and Lawrence Kohlberg described the impact of the social environment and social interactions on the ways humans change across their lifespan.

The beauty of psychological testing is that the different facets of human growth and development are included in the testing instruments. The testing instruments account for lifespan development, the field of study "that examines patterns of growth, change, and stability in behavior that occur throughout the entire life span" (Feldman, 2003). Lifespan development includes physical and psychological changes. Psychological development encompasses personality, cognition, and intellectual functioning at both the personal and social level of the individual. Whereas personality traits such as extroversion and introversion can change over time and cognitive processing skills can diminish with age, pathologies such as schizophrenia and bipolar symptoms and some personality features do not change.

But with the appropriate behavioral and therapeutic interventions as well as the necessary psychotropic medications, the symptoms of significant pathologies including schizophrenia and Bipolar Disorders might be reduced or controlled.

Of utmost relevance, the experience and knowledge of the psychologists administering, scoring, interpreting, and reporting the psychological test results determine the degree of accuracy in the psychological reports. At a minimum, psychologists who administer psychological tests must possess a doctorate degree in either clinical psychology or counseling psychology from an accredited university and have at least 2 years post-doctoral experience in administering various psychological tests to diverse group of people from different occupations, of different ages, and from different cultures. To conclude, the maxim "do no harm" continues to be relevant in the practice of psychology. In the administration of psychological tests, psychologists are constantly aware of the significance of their tasks and they ensure that they practice their profession ethically and legally so that no harm befalls their clients.

References

Anastasi, A. (1992). What counselors should know about the use and interpretation of psychological tests. *Journal of Counseling & Development, 70,* 610-615.

Bird, V. J., Le Boutillier, C., Leamy, M., Larsen, J., Oades, L. G., Williams, J., & Slade, M. (2012). Assessing the strengths of mental health consumers: A systematic review. *Psychological Assessment, 24*(4), 1024-1033. doi:10.1037/a0028983

Cook, M., & Cripps, B. (2005). *Psychological assessment in the workplace: A manager's guide.* West Sussex, UK: John Wiley & Sons.

Feldman, R. S. (2003). *Development across the life span* (3rd ed.). Upper Saddle River, NJ: Pearson Education.

Foxcroft, C. D. (2002). *Ethical issues related to psychological testing in Africa: What I have learned (so far)*. In W. J. Lonner, D. L. Dinnel, S.A. Hayes, & D.N. Sattler (Eds.), *Online Readings in Psychology and Culture* (Unit 5, Chapter 4), Bellingham, WA: Center for Cross-Cultural Research, Western Washington University. Retrieved from http://www.wwu.edu/culture/foxcroft.htm

Grocholewski, Z. (2008). *Guidelines for the use of psychology in the admission and formation of candidates for the priesthood*. Retrieved from http://www.vatican.va/roman_curia/congregations/ccatheduc/documents/rc_con_ccatheduc_doc_20080628_orientamenti_en.html

International Test Commission. (2000). *International guidelines for test use*. Retrieved from http://www.intestcom.org/upload/sitefiles/41.pdf

John Paul II. (1992). *Pastores dabo vobis: Post-synodal apostolic exhortation to the bishops, clergy, and faithful on the formation of priests in the circumstances of the present day*. Retrieved from http://www.vatican.va/holy_father/john_paul_ii/apost_exhortations/documents/hf_jp-ii_exh_25031992_pastores-dabo-vobis_en.html

McFall, R. M. (2005). Theory and utility – key themes in evidence-based assessment: Comment on the special section. *Psychological Assessment*, *17*, 312-323. doi:10. 1037/1040-3590.17.3.312

McGlone, G. J., Ortiz, F. A., & Karney, R. J. (2010). A survey of psychological assessment practice in the screening and admission process of candidates to the priesthood in the U.S. Catholic church. *Professional Psychology: Research and Practice*, *41*, 526-532. doi:10.1037/a0021546

Nevid, J. S., Rathus, S. A., & Greene, B. (1997). *Abnor-mal psychology in a changing world* (3rd ed.). Upper Saddle River, NJ: Prentice Hall

Plante, T. G., & Boccaccini, M. T. (1998). A proposed psychological assessment protocol for appli-cants to religious life in the Roman Catholic church. *Pastoral Psychology, 46*(5), 363-372.

Poston, J. M., & Hanson, W. E. (2010). Meta-analysis of psychological assessment as a therapeutic in-tervention. *Psychological Assessment, 22,* 201-212. doi:10.1037/a0018679

Sacred Congregation for Catholic Education (1974). A guide to formation in priestly celibacy. *Vatican Congregation for Catholic Education,* 4, 5

Wilkinson, L., & Task Force on Statistical Inference (1999). Statistical methods in psychology jour-nals: Guidelines and explanations. American

Psychologists, 54, 594-604. doi:10.1037/0003-066X.54.8.594

Wolber, G. J., & Carne, W. F. (2002). *Writing psycho-logical reports: A guide for clinicians* (2nd ed.). Sarasota, FL: Professional Resources.